A Note to Parents and Teachers

SAINSBURY'S READING SCHEME is a compelling new reading programme for children, designed in conjunction with leading literacy experts, including Cliff Moon M.Ed., Honorary Fellow of the University of Reading. Cliff Moon has spent many years as a teacher and teacher educator specializing in reading and has written more than 140 books for children and teachers. He reviews regularly for teachers' journals.

Beautiful illustrations and superb full-colour photographs combine with engaging, easy-to-read stories to offer a fresh approach to each subject. Each book in the SAINSBURY'S READING SCHEME programme is guaranteed to capture a child's interest while developing his or her reading skills, general knowledge and love of reading.

The five levels of the programme are aimed at different reading abilities, enabling you to choose the books that are exactly right for your child:

Yellow Level – Learning to read
Green Level – Beginning to read
Gold Level – Beginning to read alone
Ruby Level – Reading alone
Sapphire Level – Proficient readers

The "normal" age at which a child begins to read can be anywhere from three to eight years old, so these levels are only a general guideline.

No matter which level you select, you can be sure that you are helping your child learn to read, then read to learn!

LONDON, NEW YORK, MUNICH,
MELBOURNE and DELHI

Series Editor Penny Smith
Art Editor Leah Germann
Jacket Designer David McDonald
DTP Designer Almudena Díaz
Production Angela Graef
Picture Research Myriam Megharbi
Dinosaur Consultant Dougal Dixon

Reading Consultant
Cliff Moon, M.Ed.

This edition published in 2011
First published in Great Britain in 2006 by
Dorling Kindersley Limited
80 Strand, London WC2R 0RL
Penguin Group (UK)

4 6 8 10 9 7 5 3
003–DD339–Jun/2011

A CIP record for this book is available
from the British Library

ISBN 978-1-4053-7559-7

Colour reproduction by Colourscan, Singapore
Printed and bound in China by L. Rex Printing Co. Ltd.

The publisher would like to thank the following for their kind permission
to reproduce their photographs:
a=above; c=centre; b=below; l=left; r=right; t=top; b/g=background

Alamy Images: Robert Harding Picture Library Ltd 20-21 b/g, 31cr b/g. **Corbis:**
Matt Brown 26-27 b/g; Larry Lee Photography 18-19 b/g, 30cl b/g; W. Wayne
Lockwood, MD 4-5c b/g, 8-9 b/g; Charles Mauzy 5tcl b/g, 24-25 b/g; Craig Tuttle
4br b/g, 14-15 b/g, 16-17 b/g, 28-29 b/g, 31bcl b/g; Jim Zuckerman 6-7, 30cb b/g.
DK Images: Robert L. Baum – modelmaker stickers crb, br; Graham High at
Centaur Studios – modelmaker stickers tr, cl, bl; Jon Hughes 4-5c, 8-9, stickers tl,
cr; The Natural History Museum, London stickers cla; The Royal Tyrrell Museum
of Palaentology, Alberta, Canada stickers c; **Getty Images:** J.P. Nacivet 22-23 b/g,
31tr b/g; James Randklev 4c b/g, 10-11 b/g.

All other images © Dorling Kindersley
For more information see: www.dkimages.com

Discover more at
www.dk.com

Sainsbury's
Reading Scheme

Yellow Level
Learning to read

Meet the
Dinosaurs

DK

Watch out!
Here come
the dinosaurs.

Here is the scary
Tyrannosaurus
(tie-RAN-oh-SORE-us).
It has sharp teeth.

Tyrannosaurus

teeth

Here is the huge
Brachiosaurus
(BRAK-ee-oh-SORE-us)
It has a long neck.

Brachiosaurus

neck

9

Here is the tough
Triceratops
(try-SER-uh-tops).
It has three horns.

Triceratops

horn

Here is the fierce Velociraptor (vell-OSS-ee-rap-tor). It has sharp claws.

Velociraptor

claw

crest

Corythosaurus

Here is the noisy
Corythosaurus
(koe-rith-oh-SORE-us).
It has a bright crest.

Here is the small
Compsognathus
(komp-sog-NATH-us).
It runs quickly.

foot

Compsognathus

Here is the clever
Troodon
(TROE-oh-don).
It has large eyes.

Troodon

eye

19

Here is the spiky
Stegosaurus
(STEG-oh-SORE-us).
It has a small brain.

head

Stegosaurus

Here is the bird-like
Gallimimus
(gal-lee-MEEM-us).
It has slim legs
and a beak.

leg

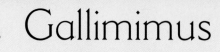

Gallimimus

beak

spike

Iguanodon

Here is the strong
guanodon
(ig-WAHN-oh-don).
It has a spike on
each thumb.

Here is the plant-eating Stegoceras (STEG-oh-SER-us). It has a thick skull.

skull

Stegoceras

Here is the armour-plated Ankylosaurus (an-KIE-luh-SORE-us). It has a tail club.

Ankylosaurus

club

29

Which dinosaur
do you like best?
The one who is…

clever?

scary?

bird-like?

spiky?

noisy?

Picture word list

Tyrannosaurus
page 6

Brachiosaurus
page 8

Triceratops
page 10

Velociraptor
page 12

Corythosaurus
page 14

Compsognathus
page 16

Troodon
page 18

Stegosaurus
page 20

Gallimimus
page 22

Iguanodon
page 24

Stegoceras
page 26

Ankylosaurus
page 28

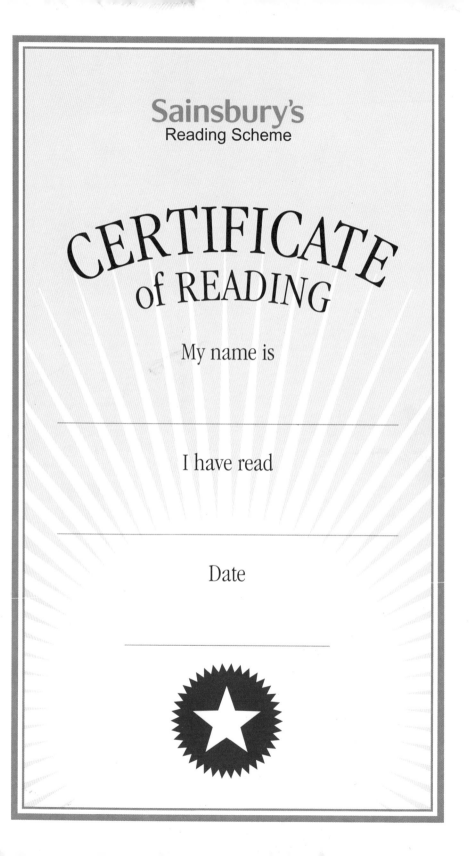

Sainsbury's
Reading Scheme

CERTIFICATE
of READING

My name is

I have read

Date